W9-AXK-881

NASHVILLE PUBLIC LIBRARY

FOUNDATION

This book
made possible
through generous gifts
to the
Nashville Public Library
Foundation Book Fund

NPLF.ORG

The Story of the
SELMA
VOTING RIGHTS MARCHES
in Photographs

David Aretha

Enslow Publishers, Inc.
40 Industrial Road
Box 398
Berkeley Heights, NJ 07922
USA

http://www.enslow.com

Copyright © 2014 by David Aretha

All rights reserved.

No part of this book may be reproduced by any means without the written permission of the publisher.

Library of Congress Cataloging-in-Publication Data

Aretha, David.
 The story of the Selma voting rights marches in photographs / David Aretha.
   pages cm — (The story of the civil rights movement in photographs)
 Includes index.
 Summary: "Explores the Selma Voting Rights Marches of 1965, including the causes of the protests, the march organizers, the violence surrounding the events, and the impact the marches had on the passage of the Voting Rights Act"—Provided by publisher.
 ISBN 978-0-7660-4239-1
 1. Selma to Montgomery Rights March (1965 : Selma, Ala.)—Juvenile literature. 2. Selma to Montgomery Rights March (1965 : Selma, Ala.)—Pictorial works. 3. African Americans—Suffrage—Alabama—Selma—History—20th century—Juvenile literature. 4. African Americans—Suffrage—Alabama—Selma—History—20th century—Pictorial works. I. Title.
 F334.S4A75 2014
 324.6'208996073—dc23
                               2013006113

Future editions:
Paperback ISBN: 978-1-4644-0421-4   Single-User PDF ISBN: 978-1-4646-1230-5
EPUB ISBN: 978-1-4645-1230-8   Multi-User PDF ISBN: 978-0-7660-5862-0

Printed in the United States of America
112013 Bang Printing, Brainerd, Minn.

10 9 8 7 6 5 4 3 2 1

To Our Readers: We have done our best to make sure all Internet Addresses in this book were active and appropriate when we went to press. However, the author and the publisher have no control over and assume no liability for the material available on those Internet sites or on other Web sites they may link to. Any comments or suggestions can be sent by e-mail to comments@enslow.com or to the address on the back cover.

♻ Enslow Publishers, Inc., is committed to printing our books on recycled paper. The paper in every book contains 10% to 30% post-consumer waste (PCW). The cover board on the outside of each book contains 100% PCW. Our goal is to do our part to help young people and the environment too!

Illustration Credits: © 1976 Matt Herron / Take Stock / The Image Works, p. 36; AP Images, pp. 20, 22, 24, 25, 26, 28, 29, 31, 32, 34, 35, 38, 47; AP Images / Bill Hudson, pp. 3, 16–17, 40, 46 (bottom); AP Images / Dozier Mobley, p. 42; AP Images / Harry Cabluck, pp. 1, 8; AP Images / Horace Cort, pp. 2, 4, 10–11, 12, 15 (top and bottom), 18–19, 46 (middle and top), back cover; Bettman / Corbis / AP Images, p. 23; National Archives and Records Administration, p. 41.

Cover Illustration: © 1976 Matt Herron / Take Stock / The Image Works (Martin Luther King, Jr., leads a march from Selma to Montgomery, Alabama, March 1965).

Table of Contents

In Selma, Alabama, whites welcomed black citizens into their stores to spend money. However, whites did everything they could to prevent African Americans from voting.

Introduction

Can you answer the following question?

The power of granting patents, that is, of securing to inventors the exclusive right to their discoveries, is given to the Congress for the purpose of _____.

The fill-in-the-blank answer is "promoting progress." But don't feel bad if you didn't know that. Virtually nobody does. Yet at one time, that was a question African Americans had to answer correctly to be able to vote in the South. White political leaders created these nearly impossible tests so that black citizens would fail them. Usually, they did.

From the 1860s until the 1960s, the American South was a segregated society. A segregated society means that the dominant racial group separates and mistreats a less-powerful group. After enslaving black Americans from the 1600s until slavery was abolished in 1865, southern whites fiercely resisted giving blacks equal rights. Whites had enjoyed the benefits of being the dominant racial group. They didn't want to give that up. For one thing, they still wanted to exploit black workers by paying them low wages.

Also, because most southern whites considered blacks "inferior," they did not want to share facilities with them. Black citizens had to attend their own schools and sit in the back of the bus. They had to use the "colored" drinking fountains and sit in the black sections of the theater. These are just a few examples of life in the "Jim Crow" (segregated) South. Because of these segregation practices, many African Americans tended to have low self-esteem. And because their wages were low and schools were inferior, most black families remained in poverty.

Southern whites also kept black people down by denying them their voting rights. The 15th Amendment to the U.S. Constitution was passed in 1870. It gave black adult males the right to vote. (Adult women would be granted that right in 1920.) But in 1876, the U.S. Supreme Court ruled that the 15th Amendment didn't *guarantee* adult male citizens the right to vote. Based on that ruling, southern politicians came up with ways to deny African Americans the vote.

Why did southern whites want to do that? Because a large percentage of the population in the South was African American. Many communities had more black residents than whites. If black people could vote, they might vote many black candidates into office. That would mean that southern whites would lose much of their power. Black leaders would want to get rid of Jim Crow laws. Without unjust laws in place, the South's segregated society would likely unravel.

Southern whites created several ways to prevent black citizens from voting. In some states, black and white people had to pay a poll tax. This meant that they had to pay a fee to the state in order to vote. Since many black people couldn't afford the tax, they did not vote. Some southern legislatures enacted literacy tests. To pass a literacy test, citizens had to prove that they could read and write. Because black schooling was so bad, many African Americans had poor reading skills. They couldn't pass the literacy test. Many low-income whites had poor literacy skills, too, but election officials passed them anyway.

Then there were the "interpretation" tests, which had questions like the one that began the introduction. Interpretation tests required would-be voters to interpret U.S. or state constitutions or local ordinances. These tests, which often were required as part of the voting registration process, were difficult. Few blacks, or whites, could pass these tests. But southern officials didn't give the test to many whites. In other cases, they helped the whites answer the questions. Or they passed a white applicant and failed a black applicant even if they had the same score. The officials' sole purpose was to deny voting rights to black citizens.

If a black person did pay the poll tax and passed a test, that meant he or she was registered to vote. But being registered and casting votes on election day had their drawbacks. Many blacks who did register were fired from their jobs. Others were threatened or harmed. In 1962, only 13 percent of black adults were registered to vote in Alabama. That number rose to 23 percent in 1964. But in Mississippi that year, it was 7 percent.

In 1957, 1960, and 1964, Congress passed civil rights acts (laws) to eliminate the voting injustice that was going on in the South. But these acts were weak. The toughest of the three was the 1964 Civil Rights Act. But even then, the only way a citizen could overcome voting injustice against him or her was to file a lawsuit. Few people had the time and money to do that.

The problem was severe in Selma, Alabama, the largest city in Dallas County. With a population of 29,500, 51 percent of the city's residents were African American. But 99 percent of the registered voters were white. On October 7, 1963, the Dallas County Voters League, led by Amelia Boynton, marched to the county courthouse to protest voting injustice in Selma. But Dallas County sheriff Jim Clark, his deputies, and members of the Ku Klux Klan (a racial hate group) broke up this demonstration. In July 1964, Clark and his troops broke up a voter-registration rally.

In 1964, Boynton urged Martin Luther King, Jr., and his Southern Christian Leadership Conference (SCLC) to stage a voting-rights campaign in Selma. Because King was such a famous civil rights figure, television cameras would surely be there. Boynton knew that when the American people saw Clark's men beating peaceful protesters, they would be outraged. That could prompt Americans to push Congress to pass meaningful voting-rights legislation.

Selma mayor Joseph Smitherman said in *Voices of Freedom*, King and the SCLC "picked Selma just like a movie producer picked a set. I mean, you would've had to seen Clark in his day. He had a helmet like General Patton."

"Jim Clark was a near madman," Andrew Young said, the SCLC's executive director, in *Voices of Freedom*. "It just infuriated him for anybody to defy his authority, even when they just wanted to vote."

King and hundreds of activists would attempt to defy Clark's authority. And he would strike back. The results would be explosive—and historic.

Chapter 1

Demanding the
VOTE

"Give Us the Ballot!"

Brown Chapel was packed on January 2, 1965. Martin Luther King, Jr., had arrived in Selma that day. Now he spoke to seven hundred African Americans. He said that the SCLC had chosen to protest in Selma because "it has become a symbol of bitter-end resistance to the civil rights movement."

Sheriff Jim Clark was the symbol personified. Clark was out of town on January 2. A day earlier, he had watched the University of Alabama football team lose in the Orange Bowl. Now, King wanted to hand Clark another loss.

In his speech, King made bold demands. If Dallas County officials didn't start registering blacks citizens to vote in large numbers, he said, he would appeal to the state government. If that didn't work, he said, "we will seek to arouse the federal government by marching by the thousands by the places of registration. Give us the ballot!" The crowd roared its approval.

Martin Luther King, Jr., makes bold declarations to the black citizens of Selma. King insisted that Dallas County officials register African Americans to vote.

Segregationist James Robinson attacks Martin Luther King, Jr., at Hotel Albert in Selma on January 18, 1965. King was not badly injured.

Marching to the Courthouse

Segregationists in the Deep South hated "outside agitators." They did not want outsiders "causing trouble" in their states, trying to change their way of life. On January 18, a segregationist attacked Martin Luther King, Jr. At Hotel Albert, James Robinson punched King in the face and kicked him in the groin. Police arrested Robinson. King, who faced violence many times during the civil rights movement, was not intimidated. The Selma campaign continued.

On January 18, SCLC leaders made their first move. Some African-American activists were sent to "whites only" restaurants and hotels, demanding service. They received service at almost every place they entered. Meanwhile, a large group of black protesters marched to the courthouse in Selma. They wanted to register to vote. Sheriff Jim Clark ordered them to wait in an alley behind the courthouse. There, they were out of view of the reporters and photographers.

These activists had been trained to protest in a nonviolent fashion. They would wait in line obediently. If attacked, they would not fight back. On this day, the Selma police did not abuse the protesters, nor did they arrest them. However, Clark issued a warning. If protesters showed up at the courthouse the following day, he declared, they would be arrested.

Sheriff Clark Strikes Back

On January 19, dozens of protesters returned to the courthouse. Sheriff Jim Clark made them stand in a long line. According to activist Amelia Boynton, he was going to lead them into the courthouse and say, "If you do this again, you will go to jail." Boynton refused to get in line or leave, so Clark went to arrest her. The photo on the opposite page (top) was pictured in America's newspapers the following day.

From January 18 to 26, Clark and his fellow officers arrested more than two hundred black activists. All had simply tried to register to vote. On January 25, Selma activist Annie Lee Cooper told Clark, "Ain't nobody scared around here."

Clark responded by shoving her. Cooper retaliated with a punch to his head. Deputies then held Cooper on the ground while Clark hit her with his billy club.

"Clark whacked her so hard," eyewitness John Lewis said, "we could hear the sound several rows back."

TOP: Sheriff Jim Clark attacks protester Amelia Boynton in front of the courthouse on January 19, 1965.

BOTTOM: Annie Lee Cooper had been fired from her job due to her activism in Selma. Here, police attempt to handcuff her after she punched Clark in the head.

Chapter 2

Hundreds of
ARRESTS

Johnson Voices His Support

The Selma campaign heated up in the first week of February 1965. On February 1, police arrested more than seven hundred protesters. Martin Luther King, Jr., and many children were among those jailed. The federal (U.S.) government responded.

On February 4, a federal judge outlawed Selma's complicated voter-registration test. Moreover, the judge ordered Selma's registrars (workers who registered potential voters) to process at least one hundred registration applications per day. President Lyndon Johnson showed his support. "I hope that all Americans will join with me in expressing their concern over the loss of any American's right to vote . . . ," Johnson told the press. "I intend to see that that right is secured for all of our citizens."

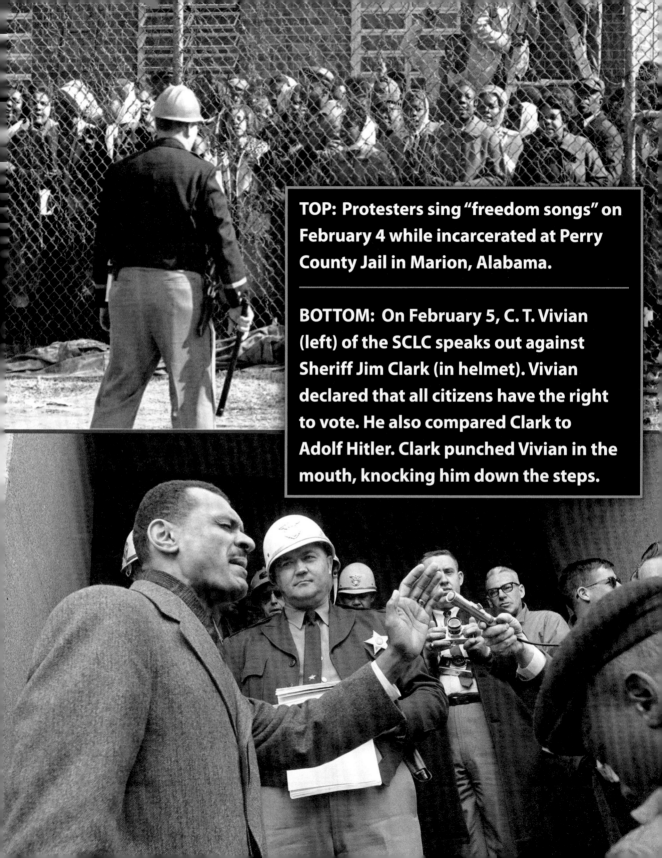

TOP: Protesters sing "freedom songs" on February 4 while incarcerated at Perry County Jail in Marion, Alabama.

BOTTOM: On February 5, C. T. Vivian (left) of the SCLC speaks out against Sheriff Jim Clark (in helmet). Vivian declared that all citizens have the right to vote. He also compared Clark to Adolf Hitler. Clark punched Vivian in the mouth, knocking him down the steps.

ONE
MAN
ONE
OPEN
THE
LET OUR
PARENTS
REGISTER
LET OUR
PARENTS
VOTE
Clark

Protesters sing and chant in front of the courthouse in Selma on February 5. Hundreds were arrested that day. In fact, by February 5, more than two thousand people filled the jails and temporary jail yards. Conditions for the activists were awful. Many complained that they didn't have toilets, only buckets. Others said that guards were abusive. That same day, the *New York Times* printed a letter from Martin Luther King, Jr. He had written it on February 1. "This is Selma, Alabama," King wrote. "There are more Negroes in jail with me than there are on the voting rolls."

Some 170 African-American schoolchildren are led on a forced march in Selma on February 10. Police made them run for more than two miles.

Forcing Kids to March

On February 10, Sheriff Jim Clark lost his composure. The sight of a hundred-plus young demonstrators outside the courthouse angered him. "Move out!" he shouted at them. Clark ordered his officers to line up the students single file on Alabama Avenue. Police then led them on a march to the outskirts of the city. A student asked where they were going. "You wanted to march, didn't you?" an officer responded. Gradually, the forced march evolved into a trot. Police prodded them with billy clubs and electric cattle prods.

A Harrowing Experience

The forced march continued for more than two miles. While police chased the students, Sheriff Clark and other officers drove along in cars. This was a horrible experience for the students. They didn't know what the police were going to do to them. For those who were not used to long-distance running, the march was exhausting. Some of the students bent over and vomited. Police eventually ended their pursuit. The next day, blacks and many whites in Selma were outraged by what the police had done. Soon after, Clark was hospitalized for exhaustion.

Chapter 3

Bloody
SUNDAY

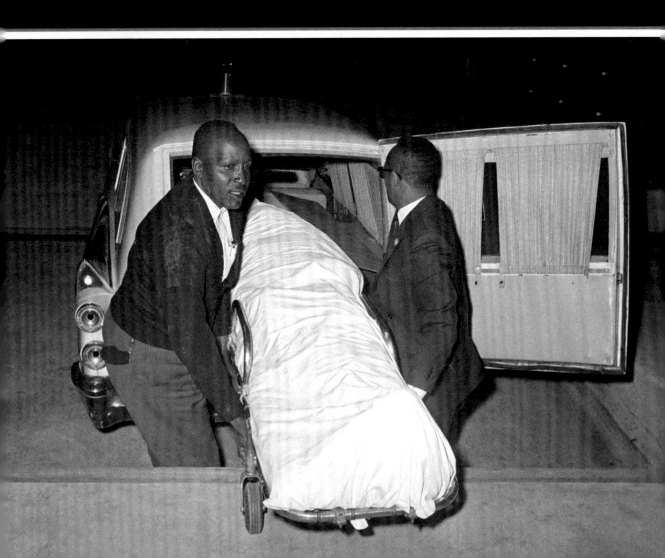

Murder at Mack's Café

By February 17, few Selma citizens had been registered to vote. "Selma still isn't right," Martin Luther King, Jr., told a church gathering. "We must engage in broader civil disobedience to bring the attention of the nation on Dallas County."

The next evening, hundreds of activists gathered at Mount Zion Baptist Church in nearby Marion. Afterward, they marched a half block to the local jail. Night marches were dangerous in the South, and this night was no exception. When the demonstrators refused police orders to go home, officers attacked them.

Police "beat people at random," Albert Turner said. "They didn't have to be marching. All you had to do was be black." Some troopers and fellow whites forced marchers into Mack's Café. The officers lost all control. They smashed lights, overturned tables, and beat up black citizens. Then it happened. Someone pulled out a gun and shot African American Jimmie Lee Jackson twice in the stomach. Jackson, age twenty-six, was a Vietnam War veteran and a deacon in a church. He died eight days later.

Jackson's death saddened and angered the African-American citizens of Selma. They became even more determined in their quest for equal rights.

The body of Jimmie Lee Jackson is placed in a hearse on February 26, 1965. That night, preacher James Bevel spoke at Selma's Brown Chapel. He announced a plan to march fifty-four miles to Montgomery, the capital of Alabama.

On March 7, state troopers told marchers to turn around on the Edmund Pettus Bridge. The marchers responded by kneeling in prayer. Troopers then attacked with billy clubs and tear gas.

Troopers Attack

SCLC leaders agreed to James Bevel's plan. On Sunday, March 7, approximately six hundred activists began to march from Selma to Montgomery. They intended to take their complaints directly to Governor George Wallace. However, they barely made it past the Edmund Pettus Bridge, which led out of Selma. A line of Alabama state troopers ordered the marchers to turn back. Then the troopers attacked them.

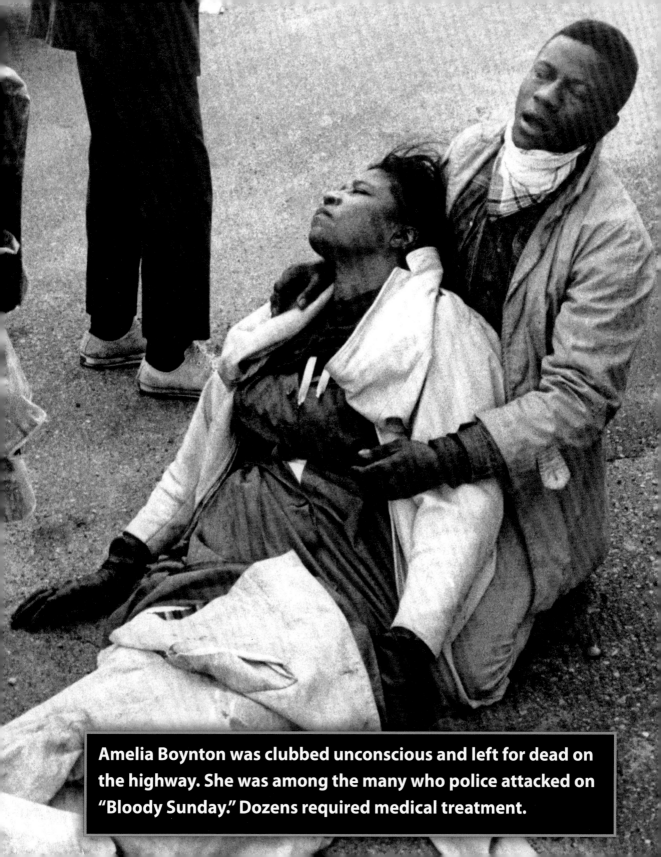

Amelia Boynton was clubbed unconscious and left for dead on the highway. She was among the many who police attacked on "Bloody Sunday." Dozens required medical treatment.

State troopers beat demonstrators near the Edmund Pettus Bridge on March 7. Film footage of the event captured the attacks of the troopers and the screams of the demonstrators.

"They're Killing Us"

State troopers, many on horseback, rushed toward the demonstrators at the edge of the bridge. Sheyann Webb, age eight, was amid the crowd on Bloody Sunday. She wrote in *Selma, Lord, Selma*: " . . . somebody yelled, 'Oh, God, they're killing us.' I think I just froze then. There were people everywhere, jamming against me, pushing me." Roy Reed of the *New York Times* wrote: "The Negroes cried out as they crowded together for protection, and the whites on the sidelines whooped and cheered." Demonstrators retreated to Brown Chapel. Some troopers followed them the whole way, still beating people.

The Nation Looks On

The TV footage of Bloody Sunday had a strong effect on Americans. George B. Leonard, who watched the events on television, recalled in *The Nation*: "*Unhuman.* No other word can describe the motions. . . . My wife, sobbing, turned and walked away, saying, 'I can't look anymore.'"

In New Jersey, a group of black and white citizens showed how much they cared. Late on Bloody Sunday, they chartered a plane and flew to Selma. That night, they were welcomed with applause at Brown Chapel.

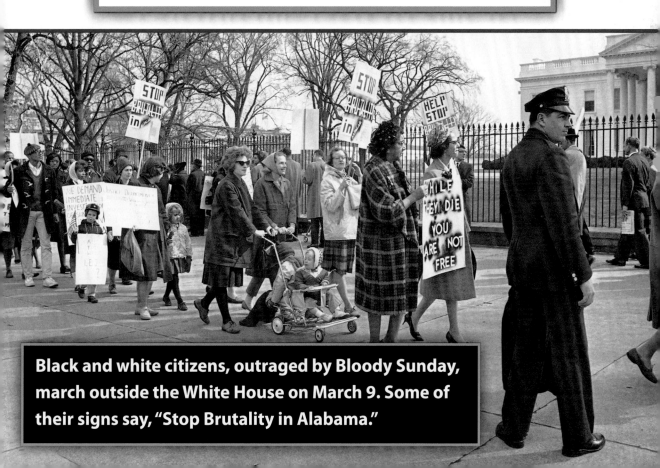

Black and white citizens, outraged by Bloody Sunday, march outside the White House on March 9. Some of their signs say, "Stop Brutality in Alabama."

On March 9, a line of state troopers awaited the marchers on the other side of the Edmund Pettus Bridge. Martin Luther King, Jr., believed that the troopers would beat the marchers if they tried to cross the line.

Chapter 4

Steps Toward JUSTICE

Turnaround Tuesday

Just two days after Bloody Sunday, demonstrators marched again toward the Edmund Pettus Bridge. A line of state troopers awaited them. But Martin Luther King, Jr., who led the march of two thousand people, did not intend to march to Montgomery on this day. He didn't want the protesters to be beaten again. Also, a judge had banned the march. President Johnson's administration had urged King not to do it. So, after crossing the bridge, demonstrators conducted a group prayer and then retreated. This march has been called "Turnaround Tuesday."

Nationwide Support

Bloody Sunday triggered a firestorm of civil rights activity. Citizens staged protests all over the country. In Detroit, for example, ten thousand people marched on March 9. Federal judge Frank Johnson held hearings about whether police could prevent Selma protesters from marching to Montgomery. President Lyndon Johnson insisted on the passage of a voting-rights bill—and sooner rather than later. The president also gave Alabama governor George Wallace a "talking to" at the White House.

President Lyndon Johnson (right) allegedly told Alabama governor George Wallace (center): "How do we want to be remembered? As petty little men . . . or great figures that faced up to our moments of crisis?"

Martin Luther King, Jr., carries a wreath during the funeral for James Reeb. A white minister, Reeb had gone to Selma to support the protesters. Hours after the March 9 protest, a group of segregationists attacked and killed him. Reeb was viewed as a civil rights martyr. In Boston, twenty thousand people attended a memorial service for him.

President: "We Shall Overcome"

On March 15, 1965, President Lyndon Johnson delivered a powerful speech on behalf of voting rights. With 70 million Americans watching on television, Johnson told southern officials: "Allow men and women to register and vote whatever the color of their skin. . . . It is wrong—deadly wrong—to deny any of your fellow Americans the right to vote in this country. . . . [I]t is not just Negroes but really it is all of us who must overcome the crippling legacy of bigotry and injustice. And we shall overcome."

C. T. Vivian of the SCLC watched the speech on TV with Martin Luther King, Jr. Vivian recalled in *Voices of Freedom*: "[W]hen LBJ said, 'And we shall overcome,' we all cheered. I looked over toward Martin and Martin was very quietly sitting in the chair, and a tear ran down his cheek. It was a victory like none other. . . ."

More good news arrived on March 17. Judge Frank Johnson ruled that Alabama police could not prevent citizens from marching. Later that day, the SCLC trumpeted the news: The third attempt to march to Montgomery would begin on March 21.

President Lyndon Johnson addresses Congress on March 15, 1965. Johnson urged members to pass a strong voting rights bill.

Martin Luther King, Jr., and his wife, Coretta Scott King, lead the march from Selma to Montgomery. No tear gas was in the air this time—only the sweet sound of "freedom songs."

Chapter 5

Marching to FREEDOM

"A New America"

On March 21, 1965, thousands of smiling civil rights supporters gathered around Selma's Brown Chapel. The march to Montgomery was about to begin. Organizers had acquired food, water, tents, and air mattresses for the five-day walk. Alabama police would not try to stop it. In fact, President Lyndon Johnson had ordered 1,800 National Guardsmen to protect the marchers. A thousand military police would assist them. At the church, Martin Luther King, Jr., declared: "March together, children. Don't you get weary, and it will lead us to the Promised Land. And Alabama will be a new Alabama, and America will be a new America!"

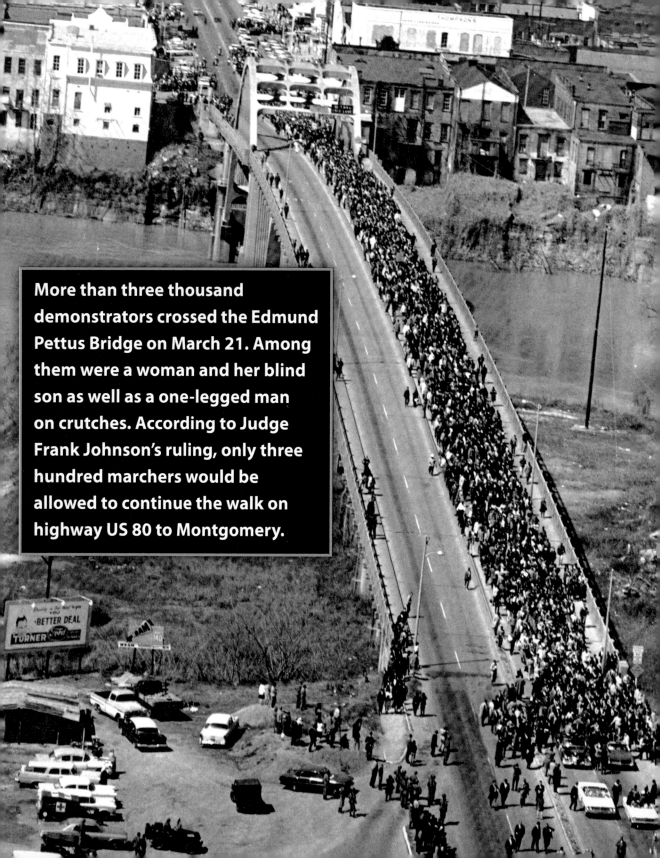

More than three thousand demonstrators crossed the Edmund Pettus Bridge on March 21. Among them were a woman and her blind son as well as a one-legged man on crutches. According to Judge Frank Johnson's ruling, only three hundred marchers would be allowed to continue the walk on highway US 80 to Montgomery.

Marcher Coleman Woodson, age seventeen, eats breakfast in the rain on March 23. Marcher Bill Bradley said in the *Chicago Defender*: "We want the right to vote, and we want it now. You white brothers can join the ranks, too. . . . Come along with us. We're going to tell brother Wallace he'll have to go."

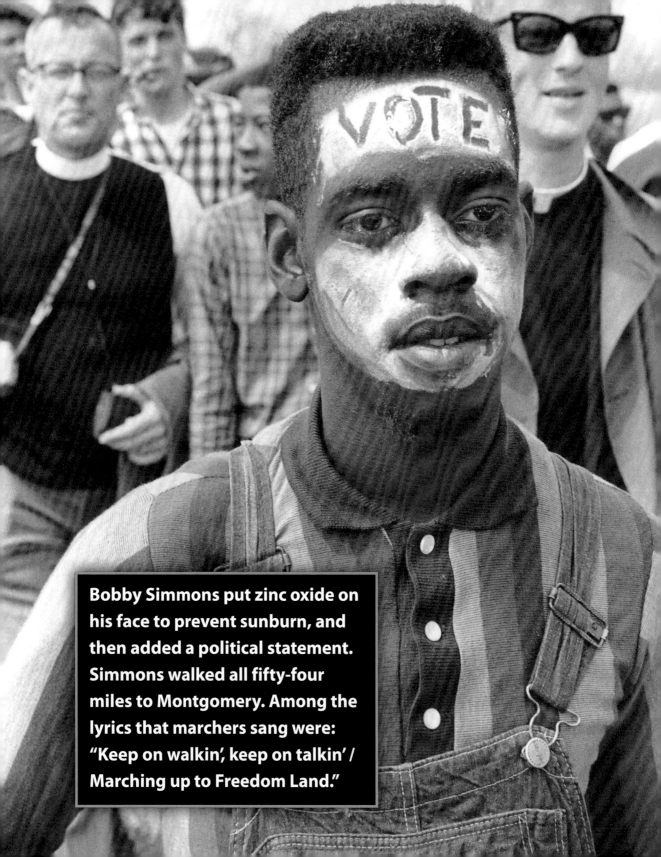

Bobby Simmons put zinc oxide on his face to prevent sunburn, and then added a political statement. Simmons walked all fifty-four miles to Montgomery. Among the lyrics that marchers sang were: "Keep on walkin', keep on talkin' / Marching up to Freedom Land."

"My Soul Still Feels Like Marchin'"

From March 21 to 25, three hundred marchers walked as many as sixteen miles a day on US 80. In addition to the grueling walk, many feared violence from the drivers who passed them. Reverend Ralph Abernathy recalled in *Voices of Freedom*: "A great deal of profanity was yelled from the passing cars." He added that "the old farmers came out, mostly white people, and they looked at us with utter disdain."

John Lewis, a young leader in the civil rights movement, described the marchers as sunburned and windburned. In *Voices of Freedom*, he said the march "was like a holy crusade. . . . You didn't get tired, you really didn't get weary. . . . To me there was never a march like this one before, and there hasn't been one since."

Eight-year-old Sheyann Webb, who had felt she was going to die on Bloody Sunday, participated in this march. In *Selma, Lord, Selma*, she recalled telling her friend Rachel: "My feet and legs be tired, but my soul still feels like marchin'." Sheyann added: "I remember standing there a long time and watching those people marching along. I would never forget that sight. And I said to Rachel, 'It seem like we marchin' to Heaven today.' And she says, 'Ain't we?'"

Chapter 6

Victory at LAST

Rejoicing in Montgomery

The three-hundred-marcher limit did not extend all the way to Montgomery. Over the last few miles, thousands joined the march. On the evening of March 24, entertainers, such as Sammy Davis, Jr., and Harry Belafonte, performed for the crowd. The next day, more than 25,000 freedom lovers gathered outside the state capitol in Montgomery. They cheered, sang, and waved American flags.

At one point, twenty Alabamans attempted to deliver a petition for voting rights to Governor George Wallace. Police turned them away. From the State House, Wallace watched the events by peeking through his window.

Civil rights leaders spoke for two hours. Martin Luther King, Jr., was the star of the show. "There never was a moment in American history," he bellowed to the crowd, "more honorable and more inspiring than the pilgrimage of clergymen and laymen of every race and faith pouring into Selma to face danger at the side of its embattled Negroes."

King concluded the speech with the lyrics of "The Battle Hymn of the Republic": "He has sounded forth the trumpet that shall never call retreat. . . . Our God is marching on. Glory, glory! Hallelujah! Glory, glory! Hallelujah! . . ." He walked away amid thundering applause.

Martin Luther King, Jr., addresses civil rights supporters in Montgomery. "Let us march on ballot boxes," he said, "until the Wallaces of our nation tremble away in silence."

Liuzzo: Killed by the Klan

March 25, one of the great days in civil rights history, ended in tragedy. That evening, Viola Liuzzo, a white civil rights supporter, gave black activist Leroy Moton a ride to Montgomery. A carload of Ku Klux Klan members shot into Liuzzo's car, killing her. The next day, President Lyndon Johnson addressed the nation about this tragedy. "If Klansmen hear my voice today," he said, "let it be both an appeal—and a warning—to get out of the Klan now and return to a decent society."

In Lowndesboro, Alabama, a large group of mourners walks to a memorial service for Viola Liuzzo. The thirty-nine-year-old Liuzzo hailed from Detroit, Michigan. She left behind five children.

Martin Luther King, Jr., and Amelia Boynton (far right) are all smiles after President Lyndon Johnson (left) signed the Voting Rights Act. The August 6 event was broadcast to the nation.

Voting Bill Signed Into Law

One year after the Civil Rights Act became law, the Voting Rights Bill was passed. More than 80 percent of Congress members voted yes for the bill. On August 6, 1965, President Lyndon Johnson signed the bill into law. The president addressed the nation, declaring: "Let me now say to every Negro in this country: You must register. You must vote. You must learn, so your choice advances your interest and the interest of our beloved nation. Your future, and your children's future, depend upon it, and I don't believe that you are going to let them down."

Selma resident Annie Maude Williams proudly holds her certificate of eligibility to vote. She received it after successfully registering to vote on August 10, 1965.

Free to Vote!

The Voting Rights Act of 1965 proved remarkably effective. Thanks to the new law, U.S. citizens no longer had to pass tests in order to vote. The act also allowed federal registrars to register African-American citizens when necessary.

In the days after the law's enactment, federal registrars flocked to the South. From August 10 to 31, they registered 27,463 black citizens. By late October, that number rose to more than 56,000. In addition, local officials registered large numbers of black applicants. From August 6 to late October, they registered more than 100,000 African Americans.

More good news arrived a year later. In 1966, the U.S. Supreme Court addressed the use of poll taxes in state elections. Since the 1800s, some southern states had required citizens to pay a tax if they wanted to vote. This fee discouraged poor people from voting. But on March 24, 1966, the Supreme Court ruled that poll taxes in state elections were unconstitutional. (Poll taxes in federal elections had been outlawed earlier in the decade.)

Throughout the South, segregationists gave up the voting fight. No longer were black citizens fired from their jobs because they registered to vote. No longer were they threatened or harassed. They voted freely and proudly . . . at last.

Conclusion

Beginning in 1966, African-American Southerners finally got to experience the "power" of the vote.

In 1964 in Alabama, only 23 percent of black citizens had been registered to vote. That number soared to 51 percent in 1966. In Mississippi, the percentage rose from 6.7 percent in 1964 to 33 percent in 1966 to 59 percent in 1968.

In the mid- to late-1960s, it was still rare to see black political candidates. However, the large number of black voters still had a strong impact on elections. Here's why: Let's say that two white candidates were running for U.S. senator in Alabama. The first candidate was a strong segregationist. The second candidate was "moderate." He or she wanted to make things better for Alabama's white *and* black citizens. In such an election, virtually no black citizens would vote for the segregationist candidate. Almost all would vote for the moderate candidate. Thus, white candidates realized that they had to be moderate—not a segregationist—to be elected.

In November 1966, black voters helped elect moderate governors in Arkansas and South Carolina. That year, even Sheriff Jim Clark tried to appeal to black citizens when he was running for reelection. One afternoon, he hosted a barbeque for black voters!

Eventually, black candidates began winning elections. By the end of 1970, 711 African Americans held elected positions in eleven southern states. That was almost ten times more than in 1965. These candidates tried to meet the needs of black citizens. Many tried to improve schools and neighborhoods for African Americans. Some tried to ensure that blacks had equal access to jobs in their cities. For black citizens, full access to voting did not lead to an immediate end to discrimination. However, it was an important step in helping them achieve more equal treatment in the South and throughout the country.

In time, African Americans won major elections. In 1973, Maynard Jackson was elected mayor of Atlanta, the South's largest city. In 1979, Richard Arrington, Jr., became mayor of Birmingham, which was once the "most segregated" city in America. In 1989, Douglas Wilder of Virginia became the first African American to win an election for governor.

In 1984 and 1988, Jesse Jackson became the first African American to run for president. Jackson, who had worked with Martin Luther King, Jr., in the 1960s, inspired minorities with his message of hope. "Hold your head high, stick your chest out," he said at the 1988 Democratic National Convention. "You can make it. It gets dark sometimes, but the morning comes. Don't you surrender!"

In 2008, Americans elected the first-ever minority candidate for president. Barack Obama, whose father was African, was elected president of the United States. He couldn't have done it without the black vote. More than 12 million African Americans voted in the presidential election in 2008, and about 95 percent of them selected Obama.

On the day Obama was inaugurated as president, a record 2 million people descended on Washington to witness the historic event. Carl Brown, a black college student, brimmed with inspiration that day. "The enormity of this moment is hitting me," he said in *The Morning Call*. "I can't believe it's real. It makes you feel like you can achieve anything you set out to do."

Such is the power of the vote.

1865–1965: After slavery, African Americans in the South are confined to segregated (separate, inferior) facilities. They are denied citizenship rights, such as voting.

1954: The U.S. Supreme Court bans segregation in public schools.

1955–1956: Martin Luther King, Jr., leads a successful yearlong boycott of segregated buses in Montgomery, Alabama.

1957: The National Guard helps black students integrate Central High School in Little Rock, Arkansas.

1960–mid-1960s: Civil rights activists stage hundreds of sit-ins at segregated restaurants, stores, theaters, libraries, and many other establishments.

1961: Activists stage Freedom Rides on segregated buses in the South.

1963: Thousands of African Americans protest segregation in Birmingham, Alabama.

1963: A quarter million Americans attend the March on Washington for Jobs and Freedom.

1964: Activists register black voters in Mississippi during "Freedom Summer."

1964: The U.S. Congress passes the Civil Rights Act. It outlaws segregation and other racial injustices.

1965: African Americans protest voting injustice in Selma, Alabama.

1965: Congress passes the Voting Rights Act, which guarantees voting rights for all Americans.

Further Reading

Books

McClaurin, Irma, with Virginia Schomp. *The Civil Rights Movement.* Tarrytown, N.Y.: Marshall Cavendish Benchmark, 2008.

Partridge, Elizabeth. *Marching for Freedom: Walk Together, Children, and Don't You Grow Weary.* New York: Viking, 2009.

Raatma, Lucia. *Selma's Bloody Sunday.* Minneapolis, Minn.: Compass Point Books, 2009.

Webb, Sheyann and Rachel West Nelson. *Selma, Lord, Selma: Girlhood Memories of the Civil Rights Days.* Tuscaloosa, Ala.: University of Alabama Press, 1997.

Internet Addresses

National Voting Rights Museum and Institute
<http://nvrmi.com/>

We Shall Overcome: Selma-to-Montgomery March
<http://www.nps.gov/nr/travel/civilrights/al4.htm>

Index